Families

Aunts and Uncles

Rebecca Rissman

Heinemann Library
Chicago, Illinois

www.heinemannraintree.com
Visit our website to find out
more information about
Heinemann-Raintree books.

To order:

☎ Phone 888-454-2279

💻 Visit www.heinemannraintree.com
to browse our catalog and order online.

© 2011 Heinemann Library
an imprint of Capstone Global Library, LLC
Chicago, Illinois

Edited by Rebecca Rissman and Catherine Veitch
Designed by Ryan Frieson
Picture research by Tracy Cummins
Originated by Capstone Global Library Ltd
Printed and bound in China by Leo Paper Products Ltd

14 13 12 11 10
10 9 8 7 6 5 4 3 2 1

Library of Congress Cataloging-in-Publication Data
Rissman, Rebecca.
 Aunts and uncles / Rebecca Rissman.
   p. cm.—(Families)
 Includes bibliographical references and index.
 ISBN 978-1-4329-4661-6 (hc)—ISBN 978-1-4329-4669-2 (pb)
 1. Aunts—Juvenile literature. 2. Uncles—Juvenile literature. 3.
Families—Juvenile literature. I. Title.
 HQ759.94.R57 2011
 306.87—dc22   2010016998

Acknowledgments
We would like to thank the following for permission to reproduce
photographs: Corbis pp. **12** (©Larry Williams), **16** (©Tim
Pannell), **17** (©Rick Gomez), **18** (©Tim Pannell), **19** (©A.
Chederros/Onoky), **23 d** (©Larry Williams); Getty images pp.
4 (Henrik Sorensen), **5** (Eri Morita), **6** (Michael Hall), **9** (Betsie
Van der Meer), **10** (Henrik Trygg), **11** (Blend Images/JR Carvey/
Streetfly Studio), **13** (Apple Tree House), **14** (David Sacks), **15**
(Blend Images/Jon Feingersh), **20** (Loungepark), **21** (flashfilm), **23
a** (Blend Images/JR Carvey/Streetfly Studio), **23 b** (Loungepark),
23 c (Eri Morita); istockphoto pp. **8** (©TriggerPhoto), **22** (©Diane
Labombarbe); Shutterstock p. **7** (©Kacso Sandor).

Front cover photograph of a family walking in the park
reproduced with permission of Getty Images (Ronnie Kaufman).
Back cover photograph of aunts and uncles reproduced with
permission of Corbis (©Larry Williams).

We would like to thank Anne Pezalla and Nancy Harris for their
invaluable help in the preparation of this book.

Every effort has been made to contact copyright holders of
any material reproduced in this book. Any omissions will
be rectified in subsequent printings if notice is given to
the publisher.

Contents

What Is a Family?

A family is a group of
different people.

People in a family are called
family members.

Family members care for
one another.

All families are different.
All families are special.

What Are Families Like?

Families can be big or small.

Families enjoy doing things together.

Who Are Aunts and Uncles?

Some families have aunts
and uncles.

Aunts and uncles are your parents'
sisters and brothers.

Your parent's sister is your aunt.
Your parent's brother is your uncle.

Some families call special friends
aunts and uncles.

Different Aunts and Uncles

Some families have many aunts and uncles.

Some families have few aunts and uncles. Some families have none.

Some people's aunts and uncles live with them.

Some people's aunts and uncles live far away.

Some aunts and uncles are young.
Some aunts and uncles are old.

Some aunts and uncles have children of their own.

If your aunts and uncles have children, they are your cousins.

Do you have aunts and uncles?

Family Tree

Grandmother — Grandfather

Aunt - Uncle

Your Parent

Aunt - Uncle

You

Picture Glossary

 **aunt** a parent's sister

 **cousin** child of an aunt or uncle

 **member** person who belongs to a group

 **uncle** a parent's brother

23

Index

Note to Parents and Teachers
Before Reading
Ask children to name different people who can be in a family (e.g., parents, grandparents, brothers, sisters, cousins). Record their answers in a list on the board. Then ask children if they know who aunts and uncles are, and how they can be related to their families. Explain that aunts and uncles are usually the sisters and brothers of parents.

After Reading
After reviewing the family tree on page 22, encourage children to draw their own family tree. If they have aunts and uncles, help the children to include them on their family tree.